To My Dear...

Oh, the Memories We've Made.

Created by Kathleen Lashier

Copyright 1996

Linkage

P.O. Box 821
Marshalltown, IA 50158

Memory Journals for Special People

Printed in the U.S.A.
G & R Publishing Co.
ISBN 1-56383-061-2

Distributed by: CQ Products
507 Industrial St.
Waverly, IA 50677
319-352-2086

This book is dedicated to Jeannie, whose old friendship provided the memories and the inspiration; and to Juniper Hill, whose new friends provided the idyllic setting in which to create.

Dear Friend,

  Among life's sweetest blessings lie enduring friendships such as ours. We have been friends for a long long time. We get together, we reminisce, and, had we the time, we would happily uncover a lifetime-myriad of shared experiences.

  Through this little book, I intend to take the time. It will be for you, then, to enjoy. But in the writing, I will first have the joy of taking a wonderful trip backward through the years. And as I journey into the memories, I will be reminded again and again that knowing you has been one of God's great gifts to my life.

          Forever Friends,

January 1
As I recall, the year our paths first crossed was

January 2

I was _____ years old and looked something like this.

January 3
You were _____ years old and looked something like this.

January 4

My very first memory of you is when

January 5

My first impression of you was

January 6
Your first impression of me was probably

January 7
This space is for a photo from the early days of this friendship.

January 8

During those early years of our friendship, one of our closest common friends was

January 9

I recall this special memory of that person:

January 10

Another close friend during the early years was

January 11

I recall this special memory of that friend:

January 12
Other common friends were

January 13

Do you remember some of the nicknames we had for each other, like . . . . .

January 14

*At that time, we all looked
kind of like this together . . .*

January 15

Do you remember when we . . .

January 16
Later on we became friends with

_____ *and*

_____.

January 17

I think we started running around with these friends because

January 18

That was when we were about _____ years old and all looked something like this together.

January 19
Do you remember when we

January 20
The wildest friend we had was

January 21
Do you remember when he/she

January 22
The funniest friend we had was

January 23
Because . . .

January 24

My current address and phone number are (hint, hint)

January 25

Just so you'll never forget, my birthday is

January 26

My birthday party that I remember most was

January 27

Your birthday party that I remember most was

January 28

Another great party was

January 29
A really awful party memory is when

January 30

A birthday cake that I remember was

January 31
Another Birthday "tradition" we enjoyed was

February 1

*A nickname your parents used
to call you was*

February 2
I think this is how you got it . . .

February 3
A nickname my parents had for you was

February 4
I think this is how you got that one . .

February 5
My parents used to call me

February 6
Because

February 7

To this day I still have something from our old days together. It is. . .

February 8

*One thing I especially remember
about your Dad is*

February 9

I really loved it when your Dad

February 10

*One thing I especially remember
about your Mom is*

February 11
I really loved it when your Mom

February 12

I didn't like it when your Mom

February 13
I didn't like it when your Dad

February 14

Do you remember on Valentine's Day when we used to

February 15
Other memories of Valentine's Day are:

February 16

When we were "going steady" with someone, we would signify it by

February 17

*As I recall, your first boyfriend
(girlfriend) was*

February 18
Do you remember when I liked

February 19

My first kiss was with

_____ *and it was*

February 20

Remember how we used to "kiss and tell"? This is what I recall about what you told . . . .

February 21

My parents would drive us crazy when

February 22
Your parents would drive us crazy when

February 23

This is what I remember most about your Grandma/Grandpa . . .

February 24

A special memory I have of your cousin (or uncle or aunt) is . . .

February 25

One thing my parents always said about you was

February 26

I was really embarrassed at your house one time when

February 27
The worst trouble I recall getting into at your house was when

February 28
The consequences were

March 1

*One of the best times I ever had
at your house was*

March 2
*One of the worst times I ever
had at your house was*

March 3

One of the best times we ever had together at my house was

March 4

I think the worst time we ever had together at my house was

March 5

The worst trouble I recall getting into at my house was when

March 6
The consequences were

March 7

One thing I always admired
about you was

March 8
Because . . .

March 9

You could always make me laugh when you

March 10

It always drove me crazy when you

March 11
I probably irritated you when I

March 12

One rule we seldom followed was

March 13

You were always better than me at

March 14
I was always better than you at

March 15

The biggest lie I ever told you was

March 16
Because . . .

March 17

I remember this about St. Patrick's Days of our youth . . .

March 18

One of the saddest moments of our friendship was

March 19

One of the truly dangerous things
we used to do was

March 20
I think we did that because

March 21

One of the dumbest things we ever did was

March 22
One of my happiest memories of our friendship is

March 23
Do you remember when

March 24

I think the best time we ever had at a friend's house was at

_____ *when we . . .*

A Gr.'s Slumber party.
Annette, Carol, Joanne, Peggy & I.

March 25

I think the worst time we ever had at a friend's house was at

<u>Joanne Alldrege</u> when we...
played 'strip poker'-- I lost
My christian up bringing. I
knew nothing about poker. Ha _ The
worst part, a neighbor of hers peered
through his upstairs window, said
he saw us. What a shock! Sure
glad I stayed under the blanket
my modesty? was in my favor.
Needless to say, we were embarrassed
Never forget Roger Brex's Name.

March 26

The bravest thing we ever did was

March 27

I used to wish that I had your

March 28
Because . . . .

March 29
We used to imagine that

March 30

Another thing we used to pretend was

March 31
The best joke I ever played on you was

April 1
*The best joke you ever played
on me was when*

April 2

*The best joke we ever played on
someone else was when*

April 3

*The first thing we always wanted to do
when spring came was*

April 4

We were never more miserable than when

April 5
Remember when we always tried
to perfect our

April 6

Probably one of my most treasured memories of you is

April 7

My favorite club or activity that we were in together was

April 8

*I think my favorite thing
I owned was my*

April 9

I think my favorite thing YOU owned was your

April 10

Remember when the <u>greatest</u> new invention was the

April 11

*Do you remember when we
were chased by*

April 12
One thing I really loved about your house was

April 13
One thing I didn't like about coming to your house was

April 14

*The meanest acquaintance we
ever had was*

April 15
Do you remember when he/she

April 16

My parents used to hate it when we

April 17

I think our favorite store to browse in was

_____ *and we liked to*

look at the

April 18

*One of my favorite spring memories
shared with you is*

April 19

Out in nature we used to love to

April 20

The hardest we ever laughed was

April 21

Do you remember a most interesting neighbor, _____ who . . .

April 22

1950's

*The outfit I thought I looked
best in was my*

Kay - Mother made a gorgeous
kelly green wool jersey dress you
loved -- it looked wonderful on
you, too. Don't you & I wish we
could get into that dress today ☺!
I don't think we fought over clothes
like Barb & me. Ha!

April 23

The outfit I thought YOU
looked best in was your

April 24

An Easter memory involving you is

April 25

One of our heroes was _____

because

April 26
I used to collect

April 27

I recall that you used to collect

April 28

Do you remember when we wore matching

April 29

Do you remember when we bought

April 30

A time when we had to stand up against odds for something we really believed in was when . . .

May 1

A May Day memory involving you is

May 2

We used to make May Baskets with

May 3

This is what we used to put in our
May Baskets . . .

May 4

*Your household pet that I
remember most was*

May 5

I remember when we hid _____

from a parent, and it was found . . . .

May 6
I thought you looked most attractive when

May 7

I thought you looked the craziest when you

May 8

A church memory involving you is

May 9

*Another special memory I have
of you is when we*

May 10

Do you remember when we were unjustly accused of

May 11
I remember what happened and how we felt . . .

May 12

The thing I remember most about your neighborhood was

May 13

The thing I remember most about my neighborhood was

May 14

I think my best talent was

May 15

I think your best talent was

May 16

Do you remember when we

May 17

A card game we liked to play was

May 18

*One thing I remember about
your bedroom is*

May 19
One thing I remember about my bedroom is

May 20
One thing I loved to do when we stayed overnight at your house was

May 21

One thing I loved to do when we stayed overnight at my house was

May 22

I used to <u>love</u> going over to

_____*'s house because*

May 23

I used to <u>not like</u> going over to

_____ 's house because

May 24

Our first shared experiences with make-up or shaving involve

May 25

Remember how curious we used to be about

May 26
A favorite parade memory is

May 27
A Memorial Day memory
involving you is

May 28

*One thing I really liked about
your brother/sister was*

May 29

A big surprise I can recall was when

May 30

As I recall, your old phone number used to

be _____ and mine was

May 31
*We used to do some fun things
on the phone, like*

June 1

Do you remember that one of my favorite toys was

June 2

I recall that one of your favorite toys was

June 3

*Do you remember when we got in
a big fight with*

June 4

The first thing we always wanted to do when summer came was

June 5

A childhood fear that we shared was

June 6
A childhood dream that we shared was

June 7

We must have known it was wrong to steal, but do you remember

June 8

I remember a picnic we went on . . . .

June 9

We showed a lot of common sense when we

June 10

We showed a lack of common sense when we

June 11

We used to show off for each other by

June 12
One "initiation rite" we had to go through was

June 13

We made beautiful music together when we

June 14

One of our most serious problems
in those days was

June 15

Remember during rain storms how we liked to

June 16

I think our favorite magazine to read back then was

June 17

Something I accomplished that made me very proud was

June 18
Something great we accomplished together was
<u>together</u> was

June 19

The clothes we were always most comfortable in were

June 20

If someone had handed us a $100 bill
back then, we probably would have

June 21
You were most insecure about

June 22
I was most insecure about

June 23

Do you remember when we made

June 24

The happiest I ever saw you was when

June 25

One of our most stupid hairstyles was called a _____ and looked something like this . . .

June 26

One of our favorite hair styles was called a _____ and looked something like this . . .

June 27

One good piece of advice you gave me was

June 28

One bad piece of advice you gave me was

June 29

My best memory of going swimming with you is

June 30

A memory that I have of climbing trees back then is

July 1

I think we used to pay _____ *for*

an ice cream cone at _____ *and*

my favorite flavor was

July 2

I think we used to pay _____ *for a candy bar at* _____ *and my favorite was*

July 3

*A memory I have with you
and fireworks is*

July 4
A memorable 4th of July was when

July 5

To keep cool in the summer we used to

July 6

*One of my favorite summer memories
shared with you is*

July 7
Do you remember

July 8
I used to envy

July 9

I think that _____ *had*

a good influence on us because

July 10

I think that _____ *was*
a bad influence on us because

July 11
A ball game memory with you is

July 12
At parties we used to like to

July 13

*One of the first movies we went
to together was*

July 14
I think our very favorite movie was

July 15
Other favorite movies were

July 16
Our favorite movie stars were

July 17
I remember some of our favorite songs were

July 18

*The best thing about growing up
in our town was*

July 19
The worst thing about growing up in our town was

July 20

We used to have a lot of fun with your brother/sister when

July 21

Our favorite hang-out was

July 22
This is what we usually did there

July 23
This is what we usually ate there

July 24

The people we usually saw there were

July 25

I think the first dance I ever went to was

July 26

One memorable high school dance was

July 27

Do you remember how we used to dance the

July 28

Another favorite hang-out place was

July 29

The curfew I remember having to abide by was

July 30

I remember doing a really mean thing to you . . .

July 31

I remember you doing a really mean thing to me. . .

August 1
A favorite sound of ours was

August 2
My memories of going to fairs or carnivals with you involve

August 3

One of the most embarrassing things we ever did in public was

August 4
This is what I remember about your bike

August 5

This is what I remember about my bike

August 6
Your car I remember most was

August 7
My best memory of that car is

August 8

Do you remember when I drove a

August 9
My best memory of that car is

August 10

I remember we used to say

"_____" *which we thought
was really naughty at the time.*

August 11

Another favorite expression of ours was

" _____ " *and meant*

August 12

Another saying or word which was popular in our youth was

"   "

_____

which meant

August 13
*The most memorable of our Friday
night activities involved*

August 14
On Saturdays we used to

August 15
On Saturday nights sometimes we

August 16

On Sunday afternoons I remember
when we used to

August 17
The most afraid we ever were together was when

August 18

*I think that our favorite season
of the year was*

August 19
Because . . . .

August 20

Here is a little limerick about me . . .

August 21

Here is a little limerick about you . . .

August 22

I remember when we were _____

and you got hurt . . .

August 23

I remember when we were _____
and I got hurt . . .

August 24

We used to play hide and seek at

_____ and my favorite place

to hide was

August 25

One superstition we always shared was

August 26

Our favorite shared book was probably

August 27

One thing we looked forward to at the start of school was

August 28

One of my "first day of school" memories is

August 29

These are the teachers I remember most . . .

August 30

The teacher that appreciated us the most was probably _____ *because*

August 31

The teacher that appreciated us the least was probably _____ *because*

September 1

The teacher I had the biggest crush on was

_____ *because*

September 2

*The best trick we ever played
on a teacher was when*

September 3

The meanest trick anyone played on a teacher was when

September 4

The worst thing I ever saw a teacher do to a student was

September 5
The thing I remember most about school lunches is

September 6
Our typical school day outfit was

September 7
The naughtiest thing I remember us doing in school was

September 8
The consequences were

September 9
A school custodian I remember was

September 10

My favorite subject in school was

_____ *because*

September 11

My favorite teacher was

_____ *because*

September 12
I think our worst teacher was

_____ *because*

September 13

I thought the smartest kid in our school was _____ *because*

September 14

I thought the dumbest kid in our school

was _____ *because*

September 15

If we could go back to our school days, do you think we would do this differently?..

September 16

I think the biggest problem I had
in school was

September 17

As I recall, you always talked about

wanting to be a _____

when you grew up.

September 18

Our school principal was _____ and this is what I remember most about him/her . . .

September 19

The worst school bully I can remember was

_____ *who used to*

September 20

One nickname given to me by classmates

was _____ *because*

September 21

One nickname given to you by classmates

was _____ *because*

September 22

Do you remember in school when we

September 23

My favorite memory of recess is when we

September 24

My best memories of getting to and from school involve

September 25
*We had several names for people
we didn't like . . .*

September 26

Do you remember when we thought

_____ *was so dumb because*

September 27
We thought it was really cool to wear

September 28

*I remember that our school colors
and mascot were*

September 29

*Remember when our cheerleaders
used to wear*

September 30

One of our school cheers went something like this . . .

October 1

*This is what I remember most
about Homecoming . . .*

October 2

This is what I remember about homework in those days. . . . .

October 3

We used to talk a lot about

October 4
We used to laugh a lot about

October 5
We used to worry a lot about

October 6
*One of my favorite fall memories
shared with you is*

October 7

We made up some great inside games, like

October 8

We made up some great outside games, like

October 9

Do you know that I still have

my _____ *from my*

childhood and I keep it

October 10

One food I remember us making and enjoying together was

October 11

Do you remember that we could

never agree on

October 12

The playground or park equipment I remember playing on with you was

October 13

Do you remember when we thought

_____ *was so beautiful,*

because . . .

October 14

Do you remember when we thought

_____ *was so exciting,*

because . . .

October 15

Do you remember when we thought

_____ *was so cool, because . . .*

October 16

The neatest shoes we used to wear were

October 17

Our parents probably watched us and said to themselves

October 18

Of all the things we ever did together, the activity that would have upset our parents most if they had known was

October 19

One thing I remember about gym class is

October 20

I remember riding with you on

a _____ *and we*

October 21

Even though we knew it was wrong, we used to make fun of

October 22

We always wanted to hurry and grow up so that we could

October 23

We sometimes wished we would

<u>never</u> grow up because

October 24
I think the hardest we ever worked together was

October 25

We used to feel quite daring when we

October 26
Do you remember when we

October 27

I think the <u>most angry</u> I ever saw you was when

October 28

Do you remember when we dressed up as _____

and we

October 29

*Do you remember at Halloween
when some kids used to*

October 30
A favorite Halloween memory

involving you is

October 31

*My memory of telling ghost stories
with you is when*

November 1

I remember when we camped out . . .

November 2

The first thing we always wanted to do when winter came was

November 3

One thing that I was always really proud of was

November 4

Do you remember when we were really startled by

November 5

The strangest person I remember living in our town was

November 6
Do you remember

November 7
I think the farthest we ever walked was

November 8

The biggest lie you ever told me was

November 9

This is what I remember about being in a play or program with you . . .

November 10

Do you remember sneaking out of the house and

November 11
The biggest fight we ever had was

November 12
People used to tease me about

November 13

As I recall, people used to tease you about

November 14

*There were some crazy nicknames
for kids in our school.
Remember . . .*

November 15

One household chore I remember you used to have to do was

November 16

A shared memory involving a war during our friendship is

November 17

If you have another photo together to share, place it here.

November 18

Do you remember how much we hated

_____ *because*

November 19
Do you remember when

November 20

Do you remember when we broke . . .

November 21

I remember this rhyme from our childhood . . .

November 22

On TV we used to like to watch

_____ *because*

November 23
A favorite Thanksgiving memory involving you is

November 24

One of my favorite winter memories shared with you is

November 25

Do you remember when _____
was watching us . . .

and we did not know it?

November 26

Do you remember when we thought

_____ *was so mean, because . . .*

November 27

Do you remember when school was cancelled because _____ and we

November 28

Do you remember when I gave you a

November 29

I remember when you gave me a

November 30
We used to love to play

December 1
Another game we played was

December 2

I think the reason we were such good friends was

December 3
*The most fun we <u>ever</u> had
together was*

December 4

As I recall, another of our favorite places to go together was

December 5
One of the nicest things you ever did for me was

December 6
Your most endearing habit was

December 7
Your most irritating habit was

December 8

I think that I was a good influence on you in this way . . .

December 9
I think that I was a bad influence on you in this way . . .

December 10
You were a good influence on
me in this way . . .

December 11

You were a bad influence on me in this way . . .

December 12

Top Ten Reasons why I have been fortunate to have you for a friend:

10.

9.

8.

7.

6.

December 13

5.

4.

3.

2.

1 reason:

December 14

Top Ten Reasons why you have been fortunate to have me for a friend:

10.

9.

8.

7.

6.

December 15

5.

4.

3.

2.

#*1 reason:*

December 16

Top Ten Reasons why we should get together more often now:

10.

9.

8.

7.

6.

December 17

5.

4.

3.

2.

#*1 reason:*

December 18

If we could take a trip together somewhere to catch up on old times,

I would choose to go to

December 19
You helped make me a better person in the following way . . .

December 20

The time came when we had to go our separate ways. We were about ____ years old and looked something like this.

December 21
The feelings I associate with that time were

December 22
I think we left our mark . . .

December 23
A favorite slumber party memory is

December 24

A value that I still carry from
our friendship is

December 25

One of my favorite memories of you at Christmas time is

December 26

I remember going _____
skating together and

December 27
Do you remember

December 28

*Another special memory I have
of our friendship is*

December 29
I enjoy recalling when

December 30
*One of my New Year's memories
of you involves*

December 31
Oh, and one last thing . . .